Life After Divorce: Finding Light in Life's Darkest Season – 8 Week Study Guide Based on the *Life After Divorce: Finding Light in Life's Darkest Season* by Dr. Scott & Leah Silverii, this guide is designed as a companion for the book and video series. Life After Divorce is available in book and workbooks for individuals, small groups and divorce care.

© 2019 by Dr. Scott & Leah Silverii

Five Stones Press, Dallas, Texas www.fivestonesu.com

All rights reserved. No part of this publication may be reproduced, stored in a retrieval system, or transmitted in any form or by any means—electronic, mechanical, photocopy, recording, or any other—except for brief quotations in printed reviews, without the prior permission of the publisher.

Most Scripture quotations are from the Holy Bible: New King James Version®. NKJV®. Copyright © 1982 by Thomas Nelson, Inc. Used by permission. All rights reserved.

Other versions used include: NASB - New American Standard Bible®, Copyright © 1960, 1962, 1963, 1968, 1971, 1972, 1973, 1975, 1977, 1995 by The Lockman Foundation.

NIV - The Holy Bible, New International Version® NIV® Copyright © 1973, 1978, 1984 by International Bible Society® Used by permission. All rights reserved worldwide.

NET - New English Translation® NET® Copyright © 1996-2006 by Biblical Studies Press, L.L.C. All rights reserved.

KJV - King James Version, Authorized King James Version, Public Domain.

Other Books and Studies by Dr. Scott Silverii

Bro, Man Up (Book and Study Guide)

Bro, Keep it in Your Pants (Book and Study Guide)

Bro, You Free?

Bro, Stay Free

Bro Code Devotional

Broken and Blue: A Policeman's Guide to Health, Hope, and Healing

Uncuffed

Study Guide
Eight Lessons

Bestselling Authors of UNCUFFED and THE BROCODE SERIES

Life After Divorce

Finding Light in Life's Darkest Season

Dr. Scott and Leah Silverii

Five Stones Press

TABLE OF CONTENTS

Introduction..8

Session 1...11
Reality of Divorce, Denial and Isolation

Session 2...18
Anger and Bargaining

Session 3...25
Depression and Acceptance

Session 4...34
FAITH, Spiritual Grounding and Soul Ties and Forgiveness

Session 5...42
Focusing on the Future and Challenges of Dating

Session 6...49
Caution: Dating Ahead, Getting Serious and Before You Say, "I Do."

Session 7...55
Marriage: God's Design and First to Final Marriage

Session 8...61
Divorce Proofing, Soul Mates and Unicorns and Final Takeaways

Acknowledgments

Leah and I want to thank the many people who have given of their time, talents and truth as we wrote Life After Divorce. We are so blessed to have you in our lives.

About Scott & Leah Silverii

Dr. Scott Silverii and his wife Leah have blended seven kids and a French Bulldog named Bacon into a wonderfully unique family. Their passion is helping hurting marriages.

They are the founders of Blue Marriage, a ministry that mentors law enforcement marriages, and they also serve on the staff at *MarriageToday*.

Scott, a retired chief of police, holds a PhD in cultural anthropology from the University of New Orleans and is working towards his Doctor of Ministry at The King's University. Leah is a *New York Times* and *USA Today* bestselling author of over sixty works of fiction.

When not spending time with family, they enjoy crossing the country on their motorcycle, and hanging out with friends in their hometown of Dallas, Texas.

INTRODUCTION

Welcome to the Life After Divorce Study Guide. We are so proud of you for taking the necessary steps to care for yourself. This is no time to feel guilty about making sure you are okay. We want you to know that you'll be better than okay because you'll be making tough decisions based on timeless advice.

This workbook, just like the book, relies on God's Word for guiding us through darkness and into the light. Allow this workbook to help reinforce what it is that the pages of Life After Divorce have spoken into your life.

In addition to the book and this workbook, we've developed a video series to help walk you through topics that might be better received from a trusted friend or mentor. This combination of resources will provide you with practical, biblically-based guidelines, insightful discussions, and life-changing applications.

As you prepare for the first session, Leah and I want to encourage you in three areas:

- **First - *Be committed*.** If you are committed to God first, you can survive anything and live a blessed life in His light.
- **Second – *Be Bold*.** Some of the discussion questions may challenge you to talk about important issues. It's normal to feel some resistance when you've been hurt or disappointed. However, it's important to acknowledge what's really going on in your heart and mind.

• **Third** - *Focus on what you can do*. Some discussion questions may present an opportunity to be critical of your ex-spouse and others. There will be times when you can honestly say how you feel about important issues. But the key to recovery is a willingness to focus on what you can do for yourself, and what you can change in you.

The bottom line is that none of us are perfect, and because you're working to restore life to the blessing God intended, doesn't mean you've failed. It means there is a blessed life up ahead.

USING THIS WORKBOOK

Each session of your workbook will include chapter summaries, fill in the blank and discussion questions. We've also included key Scripture from each chapter to center your focus on the topic.

We've included video teaching sessions streamed from a secure online environment. The sessions directly correspond with the content in this workbook. As you watch each message, you can follow along with the teaching outline in your workbook.

QUESTIONS

This section of your workbook features fill-in-the blank and multiple choice questions to help you review key themes from the teaching. Some questions will immediately invoke a memory or emotion. Don't suppress it. Allow yourself to process feelings you may not even realize you're still dealing with.

Other questions may even bring some tension or frustration to the surface. This is normal. When needed, take a break and revisit the questions later. Be committed to the process of working through this guide. Trust that the end result will be a better, healthier you.

SESSION ONE

The Reality of Divorce, Denial and Isolation

(Chapters 1 and 2)

DISCUSSION:

Going through divorce isn't easy. It wasn't meant to be easy. Actually, divorce wasn't meant to be at all. Divorce is a human creation that mirrors our separation from God. You hate it, we hate it, and God definitely hates it. But the most important thing to remember is that God does not hate you!!!

God loves you.

"Yeah, great," is often what we get in response to that, and it's understandable. We're not saying you have to jump up and down for joy (though you should because He does love you), but it's completely natural to feel temporarily let down by everyone; including God.

This is part of the recovery process. Understanding and accepting that divorce does happen, why it happened, and what you will being experiencing because it happened is vital to your coming through this healthy, strong and alive.

Becoming strong will require a process that includes phases associated with loss. We want to walk you through each phase while sharing our own experiences, (some good and some really bad) but the value of a shared witness is that you gain perspective and hope from others.

CHAPTER ONE - Reality of Divorce

Almost thirty years later, and I still recoil at the arrogance over my first marriage. We knew nothing about God, commitment, or covenants. Our priority was having a Baptist wedding and a Catholic reception. In other words, a great party. Like many couples, our wedding day was the beginning of the end for our marriage.

The past has a way of resurfacing when least expected. When Leah and I met, dated, and ultimately decided to marry, I brought baggage and pain of more than four decades—from childhood, through my first marriage, and from a career in law enforcement—to our relationship, and it suffered because I delayed the healing process.

Leah's first marriage story is very different, but ultimately ended the same way—in divorce. She shares the pain of abandonment, worthlessness, and being alone during childhood and she brought that into her first marriage. When they divorced, she was further abandoned by her support circle, and she, like many women, discovered her church had already taken sides. To say divorce had taken more than just her husband is a gross misrepresentation.

Because the word divorce gets tossed around like an entitled, social redo, we wanted to share studies, stories, and our personal testimonies to illustrate the harsh realities of becoming divorced. This section focuses on the painful, but survivable realities associated with it. Although it's difficult, planting the seeds of forgiveness and moving forward are your path back into the light.

CHAPTER TWO - Denial and Isolation

I was in denial about being in denial. Struggling to hold it together post-divorce, I poured everything I had into a dangerous career as a federal task force undercover agent. The riskier the mission, the better. Failing to understand denial left me spiritually and emotionally isolated and put my life in unnecessary peril.

Leah's struggles with denial were rooted in early childhood. To be honest, several denial-based behaviors were finally discovered and resolved after our marriage. She, too, directed her pain to outward success while denying herself the recovery from her past. The joy of becoming a bestselling author was only a bandage on a growing wound that had been denied the healing light.

We're combining our experiences to guide you toward recovery by identifying the importance of processing the reality of loss. Denial and isolation are common responses when divorce first becomes a fact. We'll walk you through the effects of emotional upheaval, as well as laying biblical foundations for weathering the impending storms.

VIDEO TEACHING WITH SCOTT & LEAH SILVERII:

Our video covers lesson 1, and we want you to think through what you read and heard. As Leah and I discussed the reality of divorce and the pain of loss, what were your thoughts? How does your experience relate or differ? Write out your thoughts, fears, victories and faith that God has in your future.
(videos accessed at www.lifeafterdivorce.info)

_____

_____

_____

_____

RELATED SCRIPTURES

So do not fear, for I am with you: do not be dismayed,
for I am your God. I will strengthen you and help you;
I will uphold you with my righteous right hand.
Isaiah 41:10

"Since this is an undeniable fact, you should stay
calm and
not do anything rash."
Acts 19:36

LESSON

Fill in the blanks from the teaching taken from chapters 1-2:

1. If you haven't figured it out already, divorce hurts more than our children, pride, or bank accounts. It hurts our very spirit because of a broken _____ with God.

2. The U.S. seems to engage in a pattern of marriage, divorce, and remarriage, or something I like to call the _____

3. I feel like we should repeat every few pages or so, but _____ does not heal all wounds.

4. People in crisis often mistakenly blame _____ for their circumstance and question why He hadn't swooped in to _____ them.

5. _____ is a defense mechanism allowing us to turn off the humanity switch for the sake of getting the job done.

6. Various models of Christian _____ support that purposefully trying to suppress emotions create an inner _____ instead of an inner connection.

7. Without the resistance against trauma, _____ is your mind's accomplice.

8. When denial becomes unnatural it may encourage you to continue with _____ or _____ behavior.

9. Fear can also restrict your natural perception and force you into having _____ where all of your options fail to clearly appear before you

10. Finding yourself single after divorce can create a confusion between _____ and alone. It's important to distinguish between the two. Because you're physically _____ doesn't mean you're lonely.

ADDITIONAL NOTES FROM LESSON ONE:

Take this opportunity to pray over and think about what was shared in this lesson. Reading is informational, but meditating over what was read becomes transformational. Write out your thoughts, observations and questions that may have come up during the lesson. Go back through the chapters, or keep this on hand as your work through the book. The time you invest in prayer will also reveal the answers or clarity that you may seek for very personal questions.

DISCUSSION QUESTIONS

1. Write out in detail your memory of the moment you first realized that divorce was going to become a reality in your marriage. Once you've written in detail, meditate over what you recall versus what you first perceived as it was happening and identify inconsistent incidents that may still be causing confusion, stress or pain.

___

___

___

___

___

___

2. Do you have lingering thoughts or regrets over the way to handled matters at the outset of your divorce? If feelings of embarrassment, guilt or shame plague you, detail in writing what those moments are and how you would've liked to have handled them differently. Then, forgive yourself for everything!

___

___

___

___

___

___

SESSION TWO

Anger, Bargaining and Guilt

(Chapters 3 and 4)

DISCUSSION:

This is a heavy lesson, and you'll move through the thickest of the process before emerging at the edge of restoration. We talk a bit about solid ground because that's what we both wanted so bad as the shifting sands of emotions, legal proceedings and custody battles raged on. You will come to a point where you feel as though you're catching traction in life. That's a great feeling, but remaining aware of your circumstances is the difference between touching a toe to the surface and truly being planted on both feet.

We'll cover each topic below, but we want you to always understand that divorce recovery is not a race. Don't compare yourself to anyone else. Especially your ex-spouse. The façade of social media is just that. It's a fake glimpse of someone else's manufactured highlight reel. Everyone hurts, but not everyone heals. Focusing on your return to joy will require you to set your blinders and your sights straight ahead toward better days.

CHAPTER THREE - Anger

I was once asked by our marriage counselor how I processed anger. My snap back was that I didn't get angry. Emotional control meant strength for me. I eventually learned there was no control in concealing emotions as I privately suffered without an understanding for the need to recover. But, once I opened myself up to the reality of suppressed anger, it was like a tidal flood from much deeper down than I ever imagined.

Leah was a peacekeeper. Adopted by older grandparents after being given up by her birth mother, she was forced into that role early in life. A dysfunctional childhood eventually led to a dysfunctional relationship that ended in divorce. Leah was denied the chance to process her anger because she was the one who held it together for everyone else. It wasn't until she learned to become a peacemaker instead of a peacekeeper that she was healed from her anger.

We want to help you understand that anger is not a sin, as long as you don't sin in your anger. Processing anger while working to recover from divorce helps you avoid suppressing emotions that may delay healing or manifest themselves in other forms of expression.

CHAPTER FOUR – Bargaining and Guilt

The sixteen years I spent in law enforcement's SWAT operations taught me much about the art of negotiation—also known as bargaining. Unfortunately, my personal life wasn't so well disciplined. The guilt of a failed marriage often tempted me to compromise who I was in exchange for easing the pain of loss.

Leah shares a mother's perspective of handling bargaining and guilt with her four young children. She made deals with herself that could never be kept. Guilt drove her to fill the void in their lives with trips, vacations, and meaningless material filler. It satiated the kids and bought her moments of peace. But Leah wasn't healing or progressing through the stages of divorce.

Bargaining is a natural response to regain a position of equality or superiority. If you're in the negotiation stage, you may be working from a deficit in the balance. We want to help guide you into a bible-based position where making concessions with an ex-spouse doesn't include losing yourself. We'll also help you make sure you're not bargaining with God for assurances that place you outside of His will.

Guilt is an unhealthy posture because it's not of God. Guilty leads to self-condemnation and shame. It's important to remember while you're dealing with feelings of guilt, that you balance them with reality and forgiveness. Sometimes in a repressed state of emotions, we unnecessarily heap guilt upon ourselves as a pity party prize. Don't linger there. Forgiveness is your ticket out.

VIDEO TEACHING WITH SCOTT & LEAH SILVERII:

Our video covers lesson 2, and we want you to think through what you read and heard. As Leah and I discussed the reality of anger, bargaining and guilt, what were your thoughts? How does your experience relate or differ? Write out your thoughts, fears, victories and faith that God has in your future.

(videos accessed at www.lifeafterdivorce.info)

_____
_____
_____
_____
_____

RELATED SCRIPTURES

"Rest in the LORD and wait patiently for Him; Do not fret because of him who prospers in his way, Because of the man who carries out wicked schemes."
Psalms 37:7

"Beloved, do not be surprised at the fiery trial when it comes upon you to test you, as though something strange were happening to you. But rejoice insofar as you share Christ's sufferings, that you may also rejoice and be glad when his glory is revealed."
1 Peter 4:12-13

LESSON

Fill in the blanks from the teaching taken from chapters 3-4:

1. Feeling lonely may cause _____, rejection, and feelings of being unwanted or unworthy.

2. It's often the shame of _____ and the desire to cut yourself off from the rest of the world that leads to the dark sensation of being alone.

3. Isolating yourself from God's _____ will exponentially increase your irrational emotions and compound your _____.

4. The bitterness, worry, stress, and unknown of _____ can linger for months, even years.

5. It's natural in times of crisis, or desperation, to accept a position of _____ and profess a willingness to change, even if you're in the right! (self-blame)

6. Never _____ or make decisions out of fear.

7. It's when we feel the decisions are no longer ours to control or influence that we move from an _____ _____ of adversarial confrontation to a more _____ seeker of concessions.

8. Failing at a _____ created by God to mirror His love for us is a huge factor in carrying guilt.

9. We can't stress how critical your _____ with Christ is at this time in your

_____ from divorce.

10. Regardless of the degree, your _____ are warranted and a _____ part of the process.

ADDITIONAL NOTES FROM LESSON TWO:

Take this opportunity to pray over and think about what was shared in this lesson. Reading is informational, but meditating over what was read becomes transformational. Write out your thoughts, observations and questions that may have come up during the lesson. Go back through the chapters, or keep this on hand as your work through the book. The time you invest in prayer will also reveal the answers or clarity that you may seek for very personal questions.

DISCUSSION QUESTIONS:

1. Are you mad? Is there anger in your soul that continues to surface at others, or yourself? Describe what it is that caused the anger, why it still persists, and when you plan to begin the process of forgiving those who caused the anger.

   _____
   _____
   _____
   _____
   _____

2. Do you feel as though you gave it your all to save the marriage? Did you have the chance to change or fight for it? What changes would you have made if given the chance or detail the changes you did make and what effect they had.

   _____
   _____
   _____
   _____
   _____

SESSION THREE
Depression, Acceptance and FAITH
(Chapters 5, 6 and 7)

DISCUSSION:

CHAPTER FIVE – Depression

Depression is so misunderstood and destructive that even after decades it's still hard to talk about. Like many others, I failed to take action to address the darkness that swallowed me. Instead, a pistol sat in my nightstand for years, waiting for the morning I couldn't endure another day.

Leah prided herself on being resilient. She was a stubborn, divorced woman who weathered the storms. She was tough and independent. No matter how deep her depression, she pushed forward. Unknowingly, her determination manifested because of the pain she'd been suppressing. Leah learned that her strength came through recovery, not resistance.

This important chapter supports well-being and maintaining the focus on a relationship with Christ for defeating the sadness that may lead you into a chronic condition of depression. We share more testimony so you'll know that you are not alone in your struggles with this darkness.

Depression is a term society has adopted, and like most things deserving of actual attention, has been overused to the point that it has become trivialized. While it's critical to accurately assess, don't misidentify the type or the source of your depression. You're going through so much right now that the last thing you need is to self-assess what it is you are actually experiencing.

CHAPTER SIX – Acceptance

I struggled for a long time before coming to a position of accepting the fact that I had failed in marriage and family. It wasn't until I learned how to forgive and bless that I set myself free from the shackles of loss. While there wasn't joy right away, there was indeed peace.

Leah had not experienced acceptance from her divorce, even during the first year of our marriage. Talk about a conflict created for a newly married couple. But she continued to work through the healing process and came to a point of asking for forgiveness and forgiving, praying for, and blessing her ex-husband, where she accepted the reality of a failed family and marriage.

Acceptance is a difficult stage because it's not always associated with happiness or excitement for moving on. We want you to think of acceptance in terms of Paul and Timothy's description in Philippians 4:11-13 as finding a sense of contentment.

> [11] *Not that I speak in regard to need, for I have learned in whatever state I am, to be content:* [12] *I know how to be abased, and I know how to abound. Everywhere and in all things I have learned both to be full and to be hungry, both to abound and to suffer*

need. *¹³I can do all things through Christ who strengthens me.*

Philippians 4:11-13 (NKJV)

CHAPTER SEVEN - F-A-I-T-H

I'm a very practical, example-driven learner. I understood what was being taught and mentored, but it hadn't stuck. Then, I began to conceptualize the FAITH model roadmap, and lightbulbs started to click. I found myself growing a deeper understanding for not only divorce recovery, but the importance of a closer walk with Christ. This simple, but very practical model puts everything into perspective for moving from hurt to healed.

Leah, on the other hand, is the creative thinker. It's the abstract musician and writer side of her personality that must absorb concepts before she's comfortable with them. When I shared my model with her, she instantly appreciated how it applied to her life. It continues to serve as a guide for our progress.

Forgive
Aim
Inspect
Transition
Heal

Our practical F-A-I-T-H Recovery Model is offered as a structured guide to help you progress through the realities of life after divorce, while growing more confident in your walk with Christ. The F-A-I-T-H model is your path through recovery during the transitioning seasons from loss to victory.

VIDEO TEACHING WITH SCOTT & LEAH SILVERII:

Our video covers lesson 3, and we want you to think through what you read and heard. As Leah and I discussed the reality of depression, acceptance and FAITH, what were your thoughts? How does your experience relate or differ? Write out your thoughts, fears, victories and faith that God has in your future.

(videos accessed at www.lifeafterdivorce.info)

_____
_____
_____
_____
_____

RELATED SCRIPTURES

"Beloved, do not be surprised at the fiery trial when it comes upon you to test you, as though something strange were happening to you. But rejoice insofar as you share Christ's sufferings, that you may also rejoice and be glad when his glory is revealed."
1 Peter 4:12-13

"For if you forgive other people when they sin against you, your heavenly Father will also forgive you. But if you do not forgive others their sins, your Father will not forgive your sins."
Matthew 6:14-15

"God did this so that they would seek him and perhaps reach out for him and find him, though he is not far from any one of us."
Acts 17:27

LESSON

Fill in the blanks from the teaching taken from chapters 5-7:

1. Your sinking _____ may have been a lingering sadness, melancholy, or clinical _____.

2. Sadness, and even depression, may visit, but you have the _____ in Christ Jesus to _____ its destructive grip.

3. The most important thing you should do after seeking a _____ with Christ is to give yourself some much needed _____.

4. Oftentimes, _____ is the most difficult part, and in no way is achieving it even guaranteed.

5. Sin is violating God's ____, so for you to try to exact justice on the sinner is, in effect, denying God His right to _____ the sinner for violating His law.

6. We know this may seem like an insurmountable task, but while it may feel like a death, it's actually an _____ to begin _____.

7. Do not leave your divorce _____ to chance, or in anyone else's hands.

8. In times of _____ or high stress, it's best to keep things ____.

9. Recovery requires taking a realistic _____ of your ___.

10. There can be no legacy of ___ while shackled to a past of ___.

ADDITIONAL NOTES FROM LESSON THREE:

Take this opportunity to pray over and think about what was shared in this lesson. Reading is informational, but meditating over what was read becomes transformational. Write out your thoughts, observations and questions that may have come up during the lesson. Go back through the chapters, or keep this on hand as your work through the book. The time you invest in prayer will also reveal the answers or clarity that you may seek for very personal questions.

DISCUSSION QUESTIONS

1. Most people either deny the suppressed or depressed feelings or they attach more meaning to sadness than would justify depression. Describe how deep your emotions slid toward darkness. Examine your periods of darkness and identify triggers that caused those feelings.

   _____
   _____
   _____
   _____
   _____

2. While acceptance doesn't necessarily mean you're happy, it more importantly means you have a sense of peace. Have you come to a season of acceptance? If so, describe how you've felt since arriving at an acceptance of your divorce.

   _____
   _____
   _____
   _____
   _____

3. Describe how each of the phases of our FAITH model had, are or possibly may affect your recovery path.

- Forgive

    _____

    _____

- Aim

    _____

    _____

- Inspect

    _____

    _____

- Transition

    _____

    _____

- Heal

    _____

    _____

SESSION FOUR

Spiritual Grounding, Soul-Ties and Forgiveness

(Chapters 8 and 9)

DISCUSSION:

CHAPTER EIGHT - Spiritual Grounding

Life with your head in the clouds may sound nice, but the truth of life after divorce requires that you find grounding so that you may begin planting deep roots once again. We all know loss through divorce, and part of that is having significant parts of your life ripped from their foundations.

Understanding the need and the way of walking through the shadow of the valley of death is a reassurance that God's got you covered. Remember, it's only the "shadow" and not the death that you are passing through. Shadows are a result of an absence of light, so this is where becoming grounded flips the switch for God's light.

Growing a reliance through a relationship with Christ was crucial in getting control of my personal life. In my deepest despair, God told me very plainly to "Be still." He wanted me to stop worrying about being alone. Almost twenty years later, He planted the seed to marry in my soul. God gave me that desire to marry about a year before I met Leah. But I knew she was there, waiting for me, thanks to my faith in Him.

Leah has always been deeply rooted in her faith and reliance upon God. It was that unwavering resilience that brought her through the death of her father and loss of her first marriage. But it was also what allowed her heart to remain obedient when God spoke words of restoration and second chances.

Significant numbers of divorced people enter the recovery process with no prior or active faith foundation. Left in a gulf without knowing where to turn, people are unaware of the power of prayer. We want to show why developing an active prayer life is crucial for moving toward complete recovery.

CHAPTER NINE - Soul-Ties and Forgiveness

Have you heard of a soul-tie? Honestly, I'd never heard of them until Leah and I began the process researching truths for recovering. We all have them, and some are like a thin spider's web while others are as strong as steel cable. They're supernatural connections and tethers to other people, places or events.

Some are positive, like the bond to your kids, but others can be a sore spot like high school bullying memories, or downright horrifying like abuse or divorce. The key is that you have the spiritual authority to sever whatever soul-ties are holding you back from moving to joy.

Forgiveness is the key to starting the process of cutting soul-ties. Because they exist in the spirited realm, God will eliminate them completely from your life. In order for Him to do anything in our lives, we must forgive others and ourselves. The other caveat is that He will not forgive us until we forgive others.

Where to begin? Forgive your ex-spouse. We mean, sincerely forgive them for everything and pray that God will bless them in coming to know Christ. We know it's weird to do this, but forgiving frees you from the offender, and allows God to cut those soul ties that have kept you in darkness.

After a very revealing prayer session, God placed it on my heart that I was still tethered to my son's mother. I spoke with Leah immediately and confessed that the soul-ties were not romantic, but the negative emotions were just as powerful and destructive, and they bound me to her. We both prayed for freedom from the forces that were able to cause turmoil between us through my son's mother's manipulation.

Leah shared earlier that when her marriage was crumbling from her first husband, she was overwhelmed by anger at the pastor's response to her outreach for help. She realized her own sin, but she also needed a calm in the storm, and she logically turned to her pastor for that. But he was unequipped to give her what she needed. He's only human.

During Leah's recovery process, she began to make a list of those she harbored hard feelings for. She began systematically forgiving and cutting soul-ties that kept her enslaved to the offenses of others. It wasn't long until she realized true freedom from her painful past.

Breaking soul-ties and learning to forgive is a crucial step in moving forward as a healthy individual, and it's necessary before a new romance can be explored. In this chapter, the reader learns what a soul-tie is and how to break them. They also learn that it's not only essential to forgive those who have hurt them in the past, but to bless them as well.

VIDEO TEACHING WITH SCOTT & LEAH SILVERII:

Our video covers lesson 4, and we want you to think through what you read and heard. As Leah and I discussed the reality of spiritual grounding, soul ties and forgiveness, what were your thoughts? How does your experience relate or differ? Write out your thoughts, fears, victories and faith that God has in your future.
(videos accessed at www.lifeafterdivorce.info)

_____
_____
_____
_____
_____
_____

RELATED SCRIPTURES

"Trust in the LORD with all your heart and lean not on your own understanding; in all your ways submit to him, and he will make your paths straight."
Proverbs 3:5-6

"Until now you have asked nothing in my name. Ask, and you will receive, that your joy may be full."
John 16:24

"Casting all your anxieties on him, because he cares for you."
1 Peter 5:7

"Therefore, there is now no condemnation for those who are in Christ Jesus."
Romans 8:1

LESSON

Fill in the blanks from the teaching taken from chapters 8-9:

1. Left unknown, people can begin to mold into a ____ posture whether justified or not, they ____ fault and consequences.

2. He (God) has a ____ for your life and there is ____ in sharing that with you.

3. You are in a _____ season of _____.

4. God is crystal clear about wanting you to live an _____ life.

5. The promise that we are ___ in Christ and ____ means we are not condemned to remain that person who caused the divorce or the person left behind in the wake of it.

6. Crying out to _____ is more important than _____ your best friend.

7. Your inability to ____ is based on the swing of emotion and not the everlasting ____ of God almighty.

8. Don't be surprised when you're ____ once you've been blessed with a renewed and lasting _____.

9. _____ is powerful, but it's a sword that cuts both ways.

10. _____ are formed in various ways, but one of the most common is through _____ relations.

ADDITIONAL NOTES FROM LESSON FOUR:

Take this opportunity to pray over and think about what was shared in this lesson. Reading is informational, but meditating over what was read becomes transformational. Write out your thoughts, observations and questions that may have come up during the lesson. Go back through the chapters, or keep this on hand as your work through the book. The time you invest in prayer will also reveal the answers or clarity that you may seek for very personal questions.

DISCUSSION QUESTIONS

1. Beginning to find yourself a little steadier in your daily walk is directly connected to your spiritual walk with Christ. Describe your relationship with God, and what it has meant and can mean in your complete recovery from divorce.

_____

_____

_____

_____

_____

2. Understanding that soul-ties are spiritual tethers connecting us to people and events that can have very negative effects on our current life, write out a list of soul ties that you need to cut in order to continue moving toward joy in life through redemptive recovery. Examples may be your ex-spouse, hurtful in-laws, maybe sexual affairs, or defiant acts that led to the divorce or occurred out of stress during the civil process.

_____

_____

_____

_____

_____

SESSION FIVE

Focusing on the Future, Challenges of Dating and Caution: Dating Ahead

(Chapters 10, 11 and 12)

DISCUSSION:

CHAPTER TEN - Focusing on the Future

I was so thankful to God for planting a seed of desire for marriage in my heart. Having been single for almost twenty years, I'd grown content with the idea of being alone, but not lonely. God also showed me that I had to focus on a future where I wasn't the center. It took adjustment, but Amen for the blessing of marriage and a blended family.

Leah's focus post-divorce had always been, and remained, on her kids and career. While on the surface it looked like she had it all together, inside, where it mattered the most, she was a wreck. Through recovery, she learned that self-care is not selfish care. It has and continues to make all the difference in her, and our, lives.

We want this chapter to remind you that focusing on yourself isn't about being selfish. It's the time to take inventory and ensure you realize the life you once knew is over. Our goal is to guide you through the transition of change, while also helping you to see that there are others who rely upon you. This is a tough time for the children, family, and close friends. Common sense and good decision-making are essential.

CHAPTER ELEVEN - Challenges of Dating

I'm going to bite the bullet on this one and confess that I was possibly the worst dater ever. Before God placed the desire for marriage, I had zero interest in dating, only in meeting women to fill a physical need. Of course, when I met Leah, I knew she was the wife God had promised, even though there were many challenges we had to overcome.

Leah, on the other hand, was not bad at dating. She refused to date altogether, but it was understandable considering how wounded she was and how public her career was. I still thank God that we connected, and despite the rocky start to our relationship and marriage, we know God has brought us through it all for a specific purpose—to show others that God still works miracles every day.

We will help you find the right answers as it relates to the possibility of returning to the dating scene. But before you head out the door, we offer practical advice for a world that has changed since you were last single. Hold tight as we share scripture and practical experience to help you navigate the challenges of starting a new romance. Proceed with caution.

CHAPTER TWELVE - Caution: Dating Ahead

Being vulnerable to someone is tough. Once you've been scarred by divorce, the natural jaded edge is always there to whisper that one question, no matter how wonderful the new relationship progresses. *"What if?"* It was especially true for me since I have a special needs son, and I'd come to understand that while people liked him, not everyone would love him or commit to caring for him. Leah never batted an eye. They connected immediately, as did her kids. It was purely God's hand at work.

Leah's level of international success as an author placed her in an odd situation of suitors. But, as I mentioned earlier, she avoided it all by avoiding them all. Still, here was a single mom with four young kids, with a high-profile career and profitability that far outpaced anything a Chief of Police would earn. Acknowledging caution was not a bad action. We talked early and often about our concerns.

Let's explore recovery now that you're secure enough to be voluntarily vulnerable to others. Decisions to enter the dating arena are often made from self-assessments, peer pressure, or cultural expectations, but we'll help you to avoid external pressures when your intuition is saying otherwise. Leah is a list maker, and we've included a great starter of ideas to consider for discussion before a relationship moves to the next step.

VIDEO TEACHING WITH SCOTT & LEAH SILVERII:

Our video covers lesson 5, and we want you to think through what you read and heard. As Leah and I discussed the reality of focusing on the future, challenges of dating and caution: dating ahead, what were your thoughts? How does your experience relate or differ? Write out your thoughts, fears, victories and faith that God has in your future.

(videos accessed at www.lifeafterdivorce.info)

_____
_____
_____
_____
_____

RELATED SCRIPTURES

"But be doers of the word, and not hearers only, deceiving yourselves."
James 1:22

"Remember not the former things, nor consider the things of old. Behold, I am doing a new thing; now it springs forth, do you not perceive it? I will make a way in the wilderness and rivers in the desert."
Isaiah 43:18-19

"But examine everything carefully; hold fast to that which is good; abstain from every form of evil."
1 Thessalonians 5:21-22

LESSON

Fill in the blanks from Scott & Leah's teaching taken from chapters 10-12:

1. If in your future you meet someone and decide to _____, please do not place your spouse _____ your kids in priority.

2. Take care of _____ first.

3. It's also wise to set _____.

4. Let your _____ be who you really are.

5. Prepare _____ for the possibility of meeting someone.

6. Do you have the _____ to attract someone worthy of your decision to be vulnerable to an _____ _____?

7. Just be aware of _____ as you move forward in a potential _____.

8. Victimizers target _____ because they have a skewed idea that you'll be appreciative of their attention, or since you've been without _____ for a while, that you must be eager to have it.

9. _____ _____ and community property settlements can be seen as easy targets.

10. _____ _____ prey on divorced parents for the easy access to their true targets.

ADDITIONAL NOTES FROM LESSON FIVE:

Take this opportunity to pray over and think about what was shared in this lesson. Reading is informational, but meditating over what was read becomes transformational. Write out your thoughts, observations and questions that may have come up during the lesson. Go back through the chapters, or keep this on hand as your work through the book. The time you invest in prayer will also reveal the answers or clarity that you may seek for very personal questions.

DISCUSSION QUESTIONS:

1. A personal inventory is a great idea right about now. It's not uncommon to neglect ourselves for the sake of the kids, friends, work, and anything we can possibly put in front of taking care of ourselves. Write out a list of self-care items that you've neglected, and prioritize each as action items to be accomplished.

___

2. Make a detailed list of what qualities and characteristics you will not accept from someone before you decide to meet anyone that might turn into a date. This may cause you to limit the pool of potential suitors, but trust us, you're better off alone.

___

_____

_____

3. We don't want to discourage you from meeting someone new, but you have to be careful these day. Caution is the key. Make a list of your most precious assets. It might be kids, cash, a home, car, real estate. Whatever it is that has sentimental or material value, write it out. Now make sure that whoever you meet or decide to date, that those assets are protected.

_____

_____

_____

_____

_____

SESSION SIX

Getting Serious and Before You Say "I Do"

(Chapters 13 and 14)

DISCUSSION:

CHAPTER THIRTEEN - Getting Serious

Although I knew Leah was going to be my wife, we still needed a period of courtship. While my heart was saying "Go for it," my head was reminding me of all the mistakes I'd made in the past. I applied the same principles we share in this book, and they helped me come to a rational decision that also honored God's gift of remarriage.

Leah is always pretty serious. I mean, really, the kids are more afraid of her than me. When momma gets upset, we all look for clear space. Of course, I'm kidding—kinda—but the point is, Leah is serious about being serious. I called it a courtship, I think she'd refer to as an intensive background check and audition. There's so much at stake on second and subsequent marriages. Neither of us were taking chances.

The euphoria of a new romance can be exhilarating. It's a new start, a new chance, and a renewed lease on life. Making empowered decisions, and having the full knowledge that they're accepting the partner God intended, is the singularly most positive aspect of this second chance at marriage. We'll help you get your head out of the stars and an eye back on God's will.

CHAPTER FOURTEEN - Before You Say "I Do"

I remember sitting with Leah in the quiet of my home when I told her we were going to get married. I asked her to pick a date so we could get it done as soon as possible. Had we placed the emphasis on a wedding instead of our marriage, I'm sure this book wouldn't have been written. In remarriages, love doesn't always conquer all.

Leah relied on her list making skills to outline anything we thought about and prayed over as we prepared to commit our lives through a marital covenant. Part of that was identifying events, people, obligations and anticipation for hurdles. Divorced couples bring baggage into their new relationship, and while they don't have to hold power over the new couple, unaddressed, they can wreak major havoc.

At this point, you might be ready, willing, and able to move forward with a new, loving relationship. It's going to be amazing, but God promised all things are possible, not that all things are easy. We'll cover hot-button topics most responsible for divorce in second marriages. We give you the tools to work through what love doesn't conquer.

VIDEO TEACHING WITH SCOTT & LEAH SILVERII:

Our video covers lesson 6, and we want you to think through what you read and heard. As Leah and I discussed the reality of getting serious and before you say "I Do," what were your thoughts? How does your experience relate or differ? Write out your thoughts, fears, victories and faith that God has in your future.
(videos accessed at www.lifeafterdivorce.info)

_____

_____

_____

_____

RELATED SCRIPTURES

"And I will give you a new heart, and a new spirit I will put within you. And I will remove the heart of stone from your flesh and give you a heart of flesh."
Ezekiel 36:26

"Every word of God proves true; he is a shield to those who take refuge in him."
Proverbs 30:5

"So now faith, hope, and love abide, these three; but the greatest of these is love."
1 Corinthians 13:13

LESSON

Fill in the blanks from Scott & Leah's teaching taken from chapters 13-14:

1. _____ isn't addressed in the bible.

2. _____ before you even entertain the notion of dating.

3. This is your chance to slow the spin, leverage _____ to your advantage, and make rational _____.

4. Fresh starts are _____, unless they're actually _____ of past poor performance.

5. Leave the _____ at the door, and allow yourself the chance to gain a new, vibrant _____ on life, love and marriage.

6. ___ is your friend, and in God's timing should be your only plan.

7. While ____ is the greatest, it's not ____ that complicates relationships in a real-world environment.

8. The biggest, reddest hot button for any couple are ____.

9. Protect your ____ and the blended family with ____ and the reality of challenges you both face going into this relationship.

10. Are you willing to ____ the kids at daycare to reenter the _____?

ADDITIONAL NOTES FROM LESSON SIX:

Take this opportunity to pray over and think about what was shared in this lesson. Reading is informational, but meditating over what was read becomes transformational. Write out your thoughts, observations and questions that may have come up during the lesson. Go back through the chapters, or keep this on hand as your work through the book. The time you invest in prayer will also reveal the answers or clarity that you may seek for very personal questions.

_____
_____
_____
_____
_____
_____

DISCUSSION QUESTIONS

1. If you're starting to get serious with someone, write out exactly what you have shared with them about your ex-spouse and the reason that marriage ended in divorce. Once written out in detail, pray over what you wrote and ask God to give you clarity about the facts so that what you are sharing with your new love interest is the truth. Too often we villainize the ex-spouse, and omit our being part of the problem. Not that we want you to carry blame, but we want you to have a clear vision of who you were then, and who you will be.

_____
_____

_____

_____

_____

_____

2. Write out your vision for a new relationship. Speak power to the blessing of God's second chance. You are God's child, so there is no reason to be shy or hesitant in praying over your vision.

_____

_____

_____

_____

_____

SESSION SEVEN

Marriage: God's Design and First to Final Marriage

(Chapters 15 and 16)

DISCUSSION:

CHAPTER FIFTEEN - Marriage: God's Design

I first failed at marriage because I simply thought it was something you did. When Leah and I married, I'd grown to understand that it was who I'd become. I think guys struggle with the idea of celebrating the covenant between spouses and God. Part of the recovery to romance process is learning to accept and become the change required to avoid making the same mistakes that lead to failure.

Leah has always understood the covenant model for marriage, and although her first marriage failed, she wasn't going to be deterred from making it the cornerstone in ours. Her faithfulness, to not only me, but to our marriage covenant has been a blessing. Despite all the statistics being against us, our reliance on a God-centered marriage has defied the odds.

In this section, we share realities that are often overlooked or completely unknown when entering into a marriage covenant and blended family scenario. Issues such as family traditions, forced sharing, and pre-existing financial obligations can become explosive with heightened tension. We'll help you get through these challenges with practical and bible-based solutions.

CHAPTER SIXTEEN - Marriage: From First to Final

Leah and I made the efforts early on to understand the key differences between first and subsequent marriages. There are so many variables that first marriages are free from and second marriages cannot avoid. Things like former family traditions, custody arrangements, prior financial obligations, and the reality of assuming child visitation schedules created long before a new marriage can present difficulties if unknown. Our commitment to God, each other, and our kids allowed us to turn obstacles into opportunities.

This chapter helps to show that are very stark differences between your first and your next relationship. Comparison kills the covenant. We want to help you see that one isn't better than the other, but that each is unique and deserves that respect.

VIDEO TEACHING WITH SCOTT & LEAH SILVERII:

Our video covers lesson 6, and we want you to think through what you read and heard. As Leah and I discussed the reality of Marriage: God's Design and first to final marriage, what were your thoughts? How does your experience relate or differ? Write out your thoughts, fears, victories and faith that God has in your future.

(videos accessed at www.lifeafterdivorce.info)

_____
_____
_____
_____
_____

RELATED SCRIPTURES

"I have loved you with an everlasting love."
Jeremiah 31:3

"Sanctify them in the truth; your word is truth."
John 17:17

LESSON

Fill in the blanks from Scott & Leah's teaching taken from chapters 15-16:

1. For marriage to be _____, you must treat the marriage as _____.

2. God created us because He ____ us even before we were conceived.

3. You and your spouse are the _____ _____ of God's design for relationships.

4. Likewise, women can grow deeper in ___ and stronger in their walk with God with the strong, _____ guidance of a spirit-filled husband.

5. The very first marriage ____ was between God, Adam and Eve.

6. _____ is accomplished much easier when thought of in terms of a ____ contract.

7. The truth is, most ____ people carry the same baggage and make the same ____ that damaged their first marriage.

8. Just because you love someone ____ doesn't mean they have to, or ever will love your _____.

9. Additionally, those _____ obligations create tension points and sometimes feelings of jealousy and resentment for the new _____.

10. Whether it's a plant or a new home, _____ marriages need anchors and reassurances that there are no ties or obligations to either _____.

ADDITIONAL NOTES FROM LESSON SEVEN:

Take this opportunity to pray over and think about what was shared in this lesson. Reading is informational, but meditating over what was read becomes transformational. Write out your thoughts, observations and questions that may have come up during the lesson. Go back through the chapters, or keep this on hand as your work through the book. The time you invest in prayer will also reveal the answers or clarity that you may seek for very personal questions.

DISCUSSION QUESTIONS:

1. Marriage is the reflected expression of God's relationship with us. How have you and your love discussed ways to show that love?

   _____
   _____
   _____
   _____
   _____
   _____

2. Make a list of the items of how your first marriage is different from your next. Use our list as a prompt, but dig deeper and include personal realities of the differences.

   _____
   _____
   _____
   _____
   _____
   _____

SESSION EIGHT

Divorce Proofing, Soul Mates and Unicorns and Final Takeaways

(Chapters 17, 18 and 19)

DISCUSSION:

CHAPTER SEVENTEEN - Divorce-Proof Marriage

Leah and I entered our new marriage with eyes, hearts, and minds wide open. There were no mystical fairytale expectations of an effortless happily ever after. But when things went sour within the first year, we were faced with no choice. I say no choice because divorce was not, and never will be, an option. We'd entered into a covenant and whatever it took to honor it and get back on track was what we'd agreed to do. God created marriage to last.

Leah introduced me to the world of marriage resources. I had no idea the number of conferences, workshops, books, videos and ministries available, just to name a few. Although God created marriage as an eternal gift, it doesn't come without effort and education. I'm thankful Leah led the way and introduced me to this world.

Marriage takes effort. This chapter covers tools, like marriage conferences and counseling, to navigate the unique challenges that being remarried brings. Through scripture and sharing of personal stories, we offer sound principles and practices for giving you the best recipes for successful second-chance relationships.

CHAPTER EIGHTEEN - Soul Mates and Unicorns

I've always been a realist, and learned my best, although most difficult life lessons, from concrete examples. Understanding that love is a choice and not an emotion has also allowed me to experience the truth that Leah is not my god. Too many people jump from one relationship to the next. Most aren't looking for love, they are looking for God. This also takes the pressure off Leah, because it's not her job to complete me. It's hers to love me, and she does it wonderfully.

Leah isn't a mystical dreamer either. I love her practical side, and when she says she chooses to love me, I understand the power of those words. I know her love isn't a fickle feeling, but an eternal decision. Dispelling marital myths is key to a lasting relationship.

Too many people rely on false assurances and mystical hopes of storybook love and soul mates. It's important to understand that people do not complete people, and to say your spouse is all that you need is to place another god before God. People, yes, even your spouse, will disappoint you. God will not. Here's how to ensure your priorities stay focused.

VIDEO TEACHING WITH SCOTT & LEAH SILVERII:

Our video covers lesson 8, and we want you to think through what you read and heard. As Leah and I discussed the reality of divorce proofing, soul mates and unicorns and final takeaways, what were your thoughts? How does your experience relate or differ? Write out your thoughts, fears, victories and faith that God has in your future.

(videos accessed at www.lifeafterdivorce.info)

RELATED SCRIPTURES

"The Lord appeared to him from far away. 'I have loved you with an everlasting love; therefore I have continued my faithfulness to you.'"
Jeremiah 31:3

"And over all these virtues put on love, which binds them all together in perfect unity."
Colossians 3:14

And now these three remain: faith, hope and love. But the greatest of these is love.

1 Corinthians 13:13

LESSON

Fill in the blanks from Scott & Leah's teaching taken from chapters 17-19:

1. There is a lack of _____ and sting of the _____ that comes with the first divorce.

2. Ground your value and marital security in God's word, not some stranger's media post.

3. When we rebel and either refuse to function in this "chain of command," then the spiritual center of marriage is replaced by a _____.

4. By divorce-proofing your marriage, both adults must accept that they were each _____, active people who now show _____ to surrender and _____ to one another.

5. If you want to know what the one thing you can do as a couple to reduce the risk of _____ is, it is _____ together every day.

6. An uncertain spouse with _____ sin may fear unintentional discovery by their spouse or may feel their Achilles heel will become a focal point that brings destruction to the marriage if old habits _____.

7. Soul mates _____ exist in a bible-based _____.

8. The "helper" God created is "____" in the original Hebrew. It literally means vitally important and powerful acts of _____ and support. Not to

complete, but to help. It's also the very same term used by God to describe the _____ ____.

9. God must be_____ in your marriage, and not in a statue on the mantel.

10. You were meant for so much more. Claim that ____ for your life today!

ADDITIONAL NOTES FROM LESSON EIGHT:

Take this opportunity to pray over and think about what was shared in this lesson. Reading is informational, but meditating over what was read becomes transformational. Write out your thoughts, observations and questions that may have come up during the lesson. Go back through the chapters, or keep this on hand as your work through the book. The time you invest in prayer will also reveal the answers or clarity that you may seek for very personal questions.

DISCUSSION QUESTIONS:

1. Is God at the center of your life? Is He the priority in your relationship? If so, write out how that looks in a real-life, tangible way. If God is not where He needs to be in your life, remain honest about it, and write out why not. Maybe you're still mad at Him over something's from your past, does your new love not recognize God or place a premium on His presence, or has life been just too world wind lately?

___

2. This last part is the easiest, and yet can be the most difficult; this is how you never divorce again – Decide never to divorce, and stick to that. Deal?

___

3. Finally, congratulations and thank you for working through this workbook. Looking at the big picture of your life at this very moment, how are you?

___

www.ingramcontent.com/pod-product-compliance
Lightning Source LLC
Chambersburg PA
CBHW080028130526

44591CB00037B/2706